D1003078

Hainault, via Newbury Park
and other broken tracks

Keith Jarrett

Copyright © 2013 Keith Jarrett. All rights reserved.
ISBN 978-1-291-37838-2

#pre-amble

I've hesitated for years. For years, I didn't think I could commit a bunch of poems to paper and pass them off as decent writing. When people ask where they can find my poems, I'll most often point to a YouTube link or my poorly-updated blog. Why would I want to crush my words by printing them? In fact, one of the poems here, 'On the Day...', argues that exact point: "Do not pull them down/And shackle them to board/Do not iron out its wrinkles". I want my words to "sprout their own microphones and speak for themselves" because they're messy and vocal.

I usually first hear a poem in my head then catch it with my fingers. After writing and performing it a few times, it morphs; chunks (dis)appear, emphases change and, as I learn it, the poem grows with me, reacts to current affairs and flows faster, easier. 'M&S' was inspired by an advert; 'I Woz 'Ere', references songs/phrases from my childhood; others use song and speech. Putting these poems in front of a mic has been part of my enjoyment, a way of re-enacting those moments.

Strangely, it also feels good compiling them here. I've included: poems I perform most (I'm honoured to hear 'Gay Poem' and 'Tell Me' have been used for schools training); poems that mention public transport most (hence the theme *Hainault via Newbury Park*); poems/drafts made up from other poems ('Crepe Paper Hats' was fun writing; the second 'What I miss...' uses cast offs from the original fifteen-minute version written for a theatre project.) Most importantly, these are all poems that have been on a stage – whether at a Slam championship, a cosy bar or a theatre – and all mean something to me. Ok, I'm done talking. Here goes.

#intros

what's your name where you from what you do?

...a new spelling of my name

For my birthday they rescued my name from a bargain bucket in Barking
too cheap to afford a new one

dog-eared and ragged, they wiped it down best they could
said I was an old soul anyway

I would have been a Lindsay Russell Daniel or Kurtis
but they gave me this one to suckle on

so I chewed, kicked and rattled it
till jazz piano lullabies tinkled out onto my baby stool

I carried it to school on my shoulder
my friends called it (Jarrett the) Parrot, Chief and Mellow Man:

it was the way its yellow eyes shut on top of class desks
I guess it was because it lacked focus.

older now, it became a pet I couldn't bear
to hear barked out on buses

I tried to drown it in the River Lea
it still skulked behind like a bad wind

my name was too dirty, too old
too much like my father

at home, I was LK Junior Daniel D
and anything but

        my name

but my name got bigger and grew claws
stretched to 5'8" tall and became solidly built

it swallowed me up and belched proudly
leaving me where I still remain: trapped inside

my name
        is now writing poetry, last I heard
tells tall tales about its origins:

far from the land of its adopted parents
far from the bric-a-brac stalls lining East London streets

it can be found tracing its roots
to some old Celtic village where it once meant something.

I Woz 'Ere

Do you remember when things were *wicked-uh-wicked-uh!*
When we was *chilling* at home with our one2one phones and chanting
wassuuuup!!
over the tuts of adult tongues
and they declared that the youth were doomed
that the young had strayed so far from the path by substituting *good* for *bad*
and *bad* for *wicked*
and soon evil would roam the Earth and the Apocalypse would come
Do you remember them days son?
bruv?
sistrin?
guv?
brer?

When you was chirpsing *bare* gals
and then blurting when you got re-jected!
Do you remember the way we used to bowl?
Do you remember when Old Skool Soul weren't all that old?
And when our older siblings decorated their mouths in gold?
And furnished their tongues with Jamaicanisms?
A *back-a-yard* drawl and a string vest stolen from Granddad's drawer
and *Karl Kani* garms
and that attitude, cheeeeeops!
Do you remember cutting your eye at me?

See, I was there
I was there sitting in the barber's chair

waiting five hours for them to weave my sister's hair

legs dangling halfway to the floor, eyes on the door

waiting to not be a child anymore so I could swing my arm back

and rock the same streets my elders claimed as their own

I was there even when you hogged the phone

and blocked the line with your dial-up-connection

I was there when the cutlery flew

and when mum warned you to take your hand of your kimbo

and show some respect

How could you forget?

Now do you remember

when we used to roll our eyes

and stifle yawns and sighs

as the old folks reminisced on their old-fashioned West Indian beatings?

Me gonna give you two big lick... just in case you did something wrong?

Do you remember when they said you had it all too easy?

Do you remember sucking your teeth and turning the volume up?

What was that song?

Something like: *Back in the day when I was young, I'm not a kid anymore*

See we were never strangers to nostalgia even back then;

even when we had not much history to speak of

we claimed it still

      cos we were cool

          we were sick

              we were ill

                    we were the lick

                        we were fit

                            and we were tick

and I was there
Even when you sent me upstairs
I peered through banisters and tiptoed on chairs
I saw over the cupboards
and right through your fears

I was there
being jooked on the arm for dropping off in church
      I was there
when you told tales of being stopped and searched
        I was there
when all your friends showed belly and gave birth
and others began to spit rhymes and reminisce about the old times
while *young man*s changed hands into *my yout*s
and *y'unnerstan*s became *two-two*s became *you-get-me*s
and while we drifted you said you would never forget me

But do you still remember your own truth?
Do you remember when the future was less than orange?
When it sat like a dot on the horizon?
When these cobwebbed tales held less than a speck of dust
and it was just us against the world on the run?
Do you remember when they insisted there was nothing new under the sun
and chided you for trying to re-invent your own wheel?
Do you remember how that did feel?
Or did you just ignore these words and let them pass through one ear
and out the other?

Do you remember when your lickle brother was just that – *little*?
Yeah, that was me!

That was me

See I was there
Tattooed initials into walls that
I woz 'ere
while you kicked time into the air
and let it fly

...And now I'm here
dusting off these memories we've recreated into legends
more concrete than the bricks
we tried to felt-tip and can spray
while the tape replayed
the junglist massive hit
that things is *wicked-uh-wicked-uh*
oh so wicked.

Split Ends (short version, draft 2)

I was manufactured far beyond
the Bow bells and past the crease
in the Thames where Eastenders credits
roll, past sausage roll sandwiches and saltfish fritters
foil-wrapped and wolfed down on the District
line like this mile ended way too soon.

I grew up in the Far East
in a place where we learnt to curse Hindi
at our teachers while threading earphones through
our ill-afforded sleeves pulsing with dancehall CHOOOONs!

The markets raised me from the back of white vans
and crooked billets with dog tracks barking their last orders
and car plants shrinking its workers to size.

I grew up at the fold of the London A-Z
in a bus depot where aspiration terminates or
its route begins depending
on which Burberry hat
you cover your headaches with.

I rose up on the backs
of cream net-curtains and terraced dreams
and Jafaican lingo
lay it on, lay it on, baby.

But my ends are split like
V signs created in playgrounds
where Sahir and Shawn and Simeon
shuffle cards behind the desk
and we all support Arsenal or Tottenham
unless we like the sound of loser
pushing on our chests.

They are split like
the bifurcated sources of the Northern line like
the edge where my tongue trips lazily over vowels
and my throat skips Ts like they were swinging rope.

#offtrackandontherails

buses trains plane journeys and life travels

Circle Line Revisited

Please forgive me if,
after having suffered vicariously
from various terror-inducing wars, generals, general strikes, genocide,
orange jumpsuits, hypocrisy, bribes, bombs, famine, lies,
live-8, live earth, live executions, sanctions, tsunamis, tax evasions, so-called
natural disasters,
own goals and then tomorrow's forecast
All fitted snugly into tonight's ½ hour sardine bulletin…

please forgive me then
if I now say
that the only reality left for me on this earth
exists within the Circle Line.

Have you thought about how many people actually go the whole way round?
Drunks… maybe tourists… or drunken tourists
and a few others… clandestine lovers
and the driver – the orchestrator – busying himself
into not getting dizzy
on this large-scale merry-go-round
where you don't collect £200 for passing *Go*.

All the other lines have a point.
Sensible people go end to end
(except for, maybe, the Jubilee, which I did, foolishly,
when I went to visit a friend in the hospital, twelve years ago
…I digress.)

Who created this genius
that mockingly challenges the patient passenger
to endure an everlasting series of signal failures,
minor delays, Major delays, with the odd natural thrown in
like waiting for the train ahead to pass?
A passenger's been taken ill
presumably for having walked along
the wrong type of snow.

All of my musings are irrelevant, I guess,
but for all the Circle Line's tentativeness
I wonder if you will share my fascination
as we pull up at Edgware Road station
because it is right here
that on just the odd occasion,
it changes destination
and leads straight down the finite path to Hammersmith.

This is, no doubt, where life begins…

Listed Buildings

She says they've opened up a new restaurant
up on one of the top floors
up one of those new supersized shiny skyscrapers that have recently risen up
in the square mile somewhere
with a perky waiter
his smile as opaque and crooked as the Thames

She says I'd like it.
If not the waiter
then, like, at least the plates
(which I imagine will be square
or, at least, oddly-shaped
and punctuated with a dot of food)

She says I'll like the *concoctions* too
a cosmopolitan or Manhattan
shaken to match the skyline
while I'm elevated half a mile high up from the floor.

I say elevated because we don't say lift these days
because we've shifted our language into globalisms
neologisms and semi-colloquialisms we used to get corrected for
like 24/7
and sometimes I need to sift through my lost vocabulary
and wonder where the words have gone
like a song eaten
up by the cassette player

chewed tape lost

to my parents' attic

static from the TV screen I used to feel

until the crown of my head went numb.

Before they complained we'd all been dumbed-down

when we were *really* young

and not just pretending

there was a never-ending stream of words

we used to parade

on the upper deck of the 123 bus

banana-yellow and painted

blue with our experimental curses

while Year 11s smoked out of scratched windows

and you and me chanted verses

from mixtapes you stole.

There are words that have long-graduated

from sink-Estate schools

queued in jobcentres

been left unemployed

 and doled out

no doubt now perched on some Essex barstool

where women dressed as schoolgirls order

vodka and lime.

I haven't actually *been* to Romford

All those years I was just passing through

somewhere between Time and Envy

just me and my portion of chips
and a shoulder bag full of dirty clothes
waiting on the Friday-night busstop
while that top-of-your-voice karaoke girl belted out
I believe that children are the future...

I felt that line
even through tinny headphones
a shivering puffa hood
and paranoia woven around my neck.
I felt my future would come in time
and the space between us,
between our worlds,
would collapse.

And perhaps, while the helpline volunteer
with the chirpy voice of unreason
chipped in that everything would one day be ok
in that consoling way professionals always do
I saw myself in the future
sporting a shiny new tower for a life
with a square mile for a job
and a wife with a smile that says home.

And perhaps, after I put down the phone
and held down a dot of a tear
and forced a laugh right back at you
for the prank that you never knew went wrong
it was then I learnt to embrace long silences

for absent words
and it was then I learnt to curse
and then I learnt to downgrade my dreams from a skyscraper
to a grave where I could bury them
along with all those redundant phrases
lost somewhere between the North Circular extension
and the Central Line.

I want you to know
there is no darker destination
than Hainault via Newbury Park
on a low battery
and an angry stomach
no flattery more odious than an insincere smile
and no square mile that I haven't trod down
in this opaque city
looking for you
and finding freedom.

I want you to know that things get better
and that Shards of glass posing as monuments
will never rise higher than your questioning soul
and that there is a skyscraper within you
as odd-shaped and crooked
as the city you roam
and that there is a banquet on the end of your tongue
a restaurant rising from deep within
which you can call home.

I want you to pull up a seat on a barstool
get comfortable in your skin
and invite your friends to feast.

I want you to elevate yourself from under the giant thumb
you've created out of East End churches
and Mockney and Jafaican
and I want you to find your own language.

Then, and only then,
will you manage to order something
out of that chirpy, gravelly voice
that you can drink.

Then, and only then,
can you bring up a laugh
that bubbles through the buildings
listed in your lungs
and break down the walls of this city
destroy the young boundaries that divide us –
the tall towers that hide our shadows –
and find me, whole.

What I Miss (in short), Dom. Rep. and London

We email, text and speak on the phone –
you ask me if I'm missing home
while I'm busy cutting up soursop and mango
and looking out the window at a cloudless sky.
A sound system van drives past blocking out my reply

Months go by and you still ask the same question
and this time it's a hurricane and lightning hits the line
or the machete man's gone crazy, or my tongue is tied
or I've fallen off the motorbike, or I'm feeling tired
and I just can't mouth the one thing I miss.
See, I never thought I'd get homesick
but there's a word that is pressed against my lips
just like the squelching of your new leather shoes on the caution-wet floor
towards the never-ending escalator at Angel;
the sound of cars and motorbikes and breaking glass next door;
young couples screaming at each other
…us screaming at each other, remember?

You email, we message and speak on the phone –
you ask me if I'm missing home
and I can imagine hearing the keys on your computer tapping
while I can barely make out the thoughts in my mind
because merengue is blasting in from the square
or someone's using my clippers to cut their hair
or there's interference coming through the phone in my ear
as you ask me if I miss... and tail off.

And I know you want to ask about us

but it's all too much

because my focus is on kids with AIDS

and dads in jail

and mums who've sold themselves

to set sail on tiny boats, with the dream of going to Nueva York –

leaving their children to fend for themselves –

and you don't understand, so I don't want to talk,

so we do the whole weather thing

the *English* thing;

I ask about the overcast skies which I have etched on my mind,

the thick sheets of grey that cloud over my memories,

the drizzle that frizzes your hair.

You tell me it's a perfect summer's day

and I don't want to believe you

while I'm in my usually 30° world

where every breeze is a blessing.

Where I am now, plucking soursop and digging up yam,

people don't yap about the weather to avoid awkwardness;

there are no bus shelters

with wishful-thinking timetables plastered on the side;

few places in which to hide:

bathrooms without locks

doors without keys

friends without personal space.

In this place where I am now
cicadas chatter away into the horizon
and old women crinkle up their faces into surprise
at who was the latest young man to die
although they only insinuate what from.
Meanwhile, the preacher from across the road
blocks the traffic with his makeshift pulpit
and sings a repentance song:
Pecador sin esperanza/ Jesucristo te ama a ti

And this part of me drifts off back to the simplicity of queuing
at out-of order ATMs,
or waiting for the bartender to catch my eye,
or working out which lines are closed on the weekend
because it's been a couple weeks since I've last seen my best friend,
ordering a double so I won't have to queue again,
double-glazing conmen, double yellow lines
and double-decker buses
with the same apparently loudmouth children on them.

But here, there is no room to think
because this is a place where children sleep next to their mothers
and hear everything that takes place under the covers;
there is no room here to deflect the questions *you* are too afraid to ask me
and I know our circular correspondence cannot last
but you still ask me what I look forward to doing when I get back
and you still question the one thing I miss about home
but I'll answer that next time, when it's your turn to phone
as my minutes are just running low.

Forked Tongue (after Sujata Bhatt), Dom. Rep.

I reckon I was fifteen.

Me and my class off to see the creators of the work we had

to be examined on.

I remember wanting to laugh when I heard, finally

the woman who was lamenting

the fact she had two tongues in her mouth

While trying to make sense of the Gujarati

I tried not to erupt

with my notorious cheeky grin.

But I was moved

seeing such a young frail thing

delivering such powerful emotion,

one she said she no longer felt.

So I wrote this last night half in jest:

I have three or four tongues in my mouth

I still can't quite be sure how many.

The one in my cheek hides behind my mother tongue

(you are still the stronger one)

Gradually you're being tied up

in other tongues

I can feel you weakening every day

Choking in the sea of forgetfulness

I struggle to describe the feeling of helplessness

Out of sync with the rhythm I knew
the streets are full of a new, louder beat
and day and night
my mind is lost in the mogollón
of bachata, merengue and regaetón,

In my dreams, my own mother speaks to me
in some strange mixture:
asking 'Have you been eating well?'
telling me 'Te extraño',
reminding me 'E'pa'lante que vamo'
All of these give way to a final cry:
'¡Dale más gasolina!'
drumming in my head
as I sit slowly up in bed

Here, even the water's mixed up:
divided between what to drink with
and what to bathe with
and in the sheer intensity of the heat
I need a drink for every one
of my divided tongues

I don't know what made me suddenly remember you
but I can't shake off the feeling
Maybe it's a foretaste of what's to come:
already, I'm forgetting words
and any identity I ever had
for five minutes

gets lost in envy for the pride

that the children have as daily they chant (¡Atención!):

Quisqueyanos valientes, alcemos

nuestro canto con viva emoción…

And I wonder if I could ever feel that back home

and I wonder what *Our Gracious Queen* would think.

Maybe my tongue is too strong to feel threatened

He runs freely and will never be put to the shame

of being a thousand times enslaved

Unlike in your case

there will never be an uprising

by my mother tongue

against the invader tongue

because I don't keep any tongues in my mouth:

my tongues are like shoes

and every time I have to choose which to use

as I go to bed I am naked,

tongue-less, descalzo

and I'm not sure whether that might be even worse

than having battling tongues fighting to gain deeper roots:

being without fixed tongue;

having loose tongues;

tongues that can slip away at any minute;

tongues that have to be kept under lock and key

lest a thief should come in the middle of the night

and leave me speechless.

#anthems

popular performance pieces

Tell me (what you believe)

Tell me what you believe
What you really, truly believe

What rights you'd fight for
Lay down your life for
What you want to strive for
Save for, (mis)behave for
Or just be brave for
Tell me what you stand for
Or what you'd sit down at the back of the bus for
Prepare to make a fuss for
Bleed for, cuss for

Tell me what you believe
What you really, truly believe

What do you have a dream for?
Or what would you lose sleep for?
Sigh for, weep for,
Starve for weeks for?
What would you take risks for?
Raise a gloved fist for?
Sit down and resist for,
Chains on the wrist for?

Please tell me what you believe
What you really, truly believe

What would you stand and block a tank for?

And receive no thanks for?

Just bullets in your chest

No peace and no rest

What could make *them* want to put you under lifelong house arrest?

Please tell me what you live for

And what you'd die for

Lie for, kill for, surrender your will for

What would you give your last resource for?

Throw yourself under a horse for?

Prepare to be jailed for?

27 years and no bail for?

Please tell me what you believe

What you really, truly believe

What would you sacrifice your life for?

Get scarred with a knife for?

Be put behind bars and risk your children and your wife for?

(That's your boyfriend, girlfriend, civil partner and siblings too...)

What can't you turn a blind eye to?

Because it ain't right to you?

Is there something that would make you go to lengths you're not used to?

Make a stand, even though you know people aren't going to like you?

Please tell me what you believe

What you want, what makes you breathe

What would you speak up for?
Is there anything you give a fuck for?

I thought so

I thought so

M&S poem (after the adverts)

This isn't just *any* poem
This is a choice selection
Of carefully-constructed words... and sounds
Consonants and vowels
Hand-picked individually and wrapped in subtle *nuances*
With the faint drizzle of the aroma of time-soaked metaphor

This isn't just *any* poem
This is a sensual poem, an essential poem
A full fat, protein-packed, saturated poem
A high carbohydrate slice of deviance, devised under the influence

This isn't just *any* poem
This is a love poem
And a *like* poem
A war poem and a hate poem
An angry... an irate poem
All neatly hand-rolled into one delicious bite-sized morsel

You could even call this a *latino* poem, compa'y
Pa' que sepa' que esto no es simplemente un poema

This isn't just *any* poem
This is one of them posh poems, one of them clever poems
That's meant to tap-dance around your head
And Riverdance around your ears

This poem was designed to entertain you
And then lure you into a false sense of complacent comfortableness
So that, finally, I can talk to you about dessert
And the disturbing trends in this *crème brûlée* world:

Babies, marinated underneath rocket attacks
Left to soak in the stale sauce of their own blowtorched mothers
Or how about this?
Young men left to sweat it out in their orange jumpsuit skins
Serving time (still) unknown
And something else you should never try at home
But nevertheless happens right here inside our very own kitchens
Young children left to simmer in detention centres for months, pending their exportation

But adding all of these raw, random, sour ingredients to the mix at such a late stage
Would undoubtedly unsettle the stomach
And would prove to be virtually indigestible
So, for the moment, I would like to declare this poem
Utterly unsuitable for consumption

On the day you come to wash

On the day you come to wash my words

You must rinse thoroughly in my idiom

You must meticulously follow the demands of my labels

And observe all instructions

Rule one:

My words must be washed cold and scrubbed in syncretic tongue

No demeaning chemical dry-cleaning

Just allow them the space to bathe in the polluted waters of River Thames

And the history of the Caribbean Sea

Rule one:

My words must be hand-wrung

Drawn out from hot-like-fire blood

Not made to bounce along in some mechanical drum

Let them dry freely in skyscraper sun

Not pegged to the back of some anonymous (under)line

And may they never spin

Rule one:

Let my words never come undone

But let them hang

And when they hang, may they never be buttoned up

Zipped up, *velcroed* down

Let them hang freely on wind-chapped lips

Let them pile up on chip-stacked shoulders

And on highly-strung hips

Rule one:

When my words are hung and dry

And blowing in the London sky

Do not pull them down

And shackle them to board

Do not iron out its wrinkles

Press out its creases

Tease out its kinks and loose threads

Until they are flat and dead

Do not stiffen them with your stale starchy spray

Nor surround them in moth balls

Or muffle them in cloth bags

Rule one again (for there is only one rule):

When my words are clean

When they are shiny and sparkling and fresh

Just leave them

Leave them to dirty again in exhaust-fume streets

And drain-clogged alleys

Let them ripen in work-sweat hands

And in thirsty mouths

Allow them to be *graffitied* in pidgin-English walls

And trampled on commuter-laden floors

On the day you come to wash my words

Allow them to stain and chip and grime

Allow them to rhyme

Allow them to flow

Allow them to grow organically

And let them park themselves on dirty grey pavements

And let them rot on forgotten park benches

And let them fester on draining boards until they foster fungal spores

Until they ferment and breed micro-organisms

So they can sprout their own microphones and speak for themselves

On the day you come to wash my words

I hope they are strong enough

To have built themselves a fortress around your arrogance

I hope that they are wise enough

To withstand your feeble potions

Your detergents, conditioners, lotions,

Your angry white-washing bleaches and hum-dumb driers

May they have blown far from your colonising reach

And now may they come to wash *you*

Cleanse you

Clean you

Baptise you

Intoxicate you

Detain you

And take you

Away

BHM

When they tell you this is Black history
What do they mean?
Do they mean this is history without the whitewash?
Without the grey areas or red herrings – just one big old black hole
For school kids to sink kissing teeth into?

When they tell you it's a black history they wanna teach
Of what do they speak? And what do *you* seek?
Another Windrush square for brown rears to park on grey benches?
Another bronze Mandela statue for tourist cameras to capture
And tag on Facebook and Instagram?
Or maybe this *his*tory is not a man
But a Seacole, a Parks or a disputed Nefertiti
Unearthed from out of the long lines of long-necked African Queens
and tall pyramids
And crossings-out on buried textbooks
And complex theories put out of context
Until the history is no longer black but murky and unclear...

When they tell you this is Black History
What is it you want to hear?
Is it carnival steel pan music?
Or the slosh of a slave ship treading Atlantic waters?
Or the slash of backra's whip on the backs of his own daughters?
Or freshly-slaughtered flying fish sizzling in fry pan?
Or plantain or ackee or yam?
Or the thread that connects them with fufu and jollof and egusi soup?

Is it the languages silenced

Or the violence from which they survived?

Is it the clans, the classes, the tribes that thrive?

Is it the many-hued skins that decorate walls come October?

Or the sobering lessons they teach? And Dr King's *I have a dream* speech?

When they tell you this is black history what should this inspire?

Several rounds of kum-by-yahs fired from the mouths

Of cross-legged children in damp halls?

Or the applause from parents proud to dress in newly dusted-off dashikis?

Or that dreadlock wrapped around a bald-patch?

Or a catch-all catechism

We roll out once a year so black is seen to be respected?

Tell me again, what do they mean when they say *black* history?

And what do *you* expect to learn?

Your name... in the Ghanaian way?

Kofi for Friday or Kwame for Saturday

And someday you might get to grips with the way it sounds

But for now, they have pronounced that this is black history

For now, what do they mean with this mystery of this name for this month?

Because black is infinite

And history is never over

But this is something we must muse over come October

And while libraries are open and minds are too

I want to know what this month means to you...

A Gay Poem

They asked if I had a gay poem
And I said, straight up, no
My poems don't deviate between straight lines
My poems don't *mince* their words
Or bend, or make *queer* little observations

They asked me if I had a gay poem
So I answered honestly
That, no, I don't have any gay poetry
And even if, unthinkably, I did
What would that say about me?

I mean, even presenting this question
Puts me in a precarious position
And how would I broach the subject
With my own creation?

Like: *"Excuse me... poem... are you gay?*
Have you grown up contrarily to what I wanted you to say?
I mean, I certainly didn't write you that way...
Was it something I said, something I did
That turned you? Maybe I should have peppered your verses with sport
Girls and beer
Maybe as your author I deserted you?
Or did another writer make you queer?"

Ok, let's just say, hypothetically, that *this* poem is gay

Maybe it's a confused poem that just needs straightening out

Maybe I could insert verses from Leviticus

Speak over it in tongues

Douse it in holy water

Recite it the Qur'an

Give it a beat, beat, beat

Boom box blasting in the street

Batty poem fi dead

Batty poem fi dead

Rip up chi chi poem inna shred

They asked me if I had a gay poem

And I said no

But the truth is, I didn't know

Until one of my own poems spoke up and tapped me on the shoulder

It said to me: "Look here dad/author, I'm now that much bolder

And I'm not confused, not alternative

And even though the words I choose to marry with

Make me different

It doesn't make me any less eloquent

I don't need to be overly elegant

Maybe that's why I slipped under your gaydar

But why are you so afraid to embrace it?

Face it, it's a part of me, you can't erase it

The more you try to label me with your twisted synonyms

The more you say you hate the sinner and despise the sin

The more you try to clip my words and stifle my expression

The more I know it's you, not me, whose morality should be called into question"

They asked me if I could read out a poem

They said choose one of your strongest

One of your best

Choose a poem that doesn't stand for any foolishness

They asked me if I had a gay poem

So I, proudly, said yes.

#remixes and B-sides

Experiments extras and reincarnations

What I Miss (in between the lines)

Email/Message:
Remember Liverpool St Station where, eyes closed, you said you could discern between the indifferent ruffle of a broadminded broadsheet and the scandalized turning of a tabloid reader?

A stifled cough... a private phone conversation made way too public until it is cut off... and in the blackness of the tunnel we can see into the silence.

There are journeys I take in my dreams, where I hear the squelching of your new leather shoes on the caution-wet floor towards the never-ending escalator at Angel... and a confused Babelic panic searching for tickets and maps and phrasebooks in high-pitched squeals just like the train you got off.

We stroll through parks and zig-zag through medium-sized towers which conceal university libraries, where you can just make out Centrepoint in the distance in case you get drunk in all that noise pollution and can't find your way back to the dorm.

Ok. I'll stop.

Phone:
I know you want to ask about us but right now the weather hangs on my mind like yesterday's y-fronts on the line. You tell me it's a perfect summer's day, while here, it sounds like a symphony of steel drums

Mother nature conducts the unruly band, rain thumps down on my corrugated ceiling, plus the persistent zipping of mosquitoes in my ear like plantains sizzling in a pan…

Hold on, those are my plantains and my pan! The neighbours are cooking it on my oven, in my room... just one minute... I'll call you again soon!

Message:
Ok, tell me I'm contradicting myself and that the diesel of bus fumes has got to my brain; that the big city is buzzing with the drilling of roads and sounding of sirens, and clacking of heels over cracks in the pavement.

I'll tell you there's a loudness here that doesn't exist in London, while you say my memory needs to be re-jigged.

Even though you think it's a joke I joke, I miss the silence of the Smoke.

Email:
So what about this cultural hodgepodge that was meant to bring about a furious mixture of bloody chaos? What happened to the volume of a Brick-lane curry? The blaring racket of a Brixton bashment party? The din of a thousand languages neatly queuing up just to have their say... in the job market?

Back where you are, rarely will a stranger be so daring as to offer a greeting beyond a smile... while here, there are no strangers, only neighbours – *vecinos* –, friends with egos full enough to disturb my sleep and sit on my bed and tell me stories that I won't dare to repeat.

Silence.

The messages get longer, my pull is getting stronger for home... something is leading me back to the land I said I'd never see again as you ask me if by silence *I mean* privacy, *and I answer* I'm not sure – *but boundaries don't exist here anymore.*

Email:

And this tiny part of me drifts off back to the simplicity of queuing
at out-of order cashpoints, or double glazing conmen, double yellow lines and
double-decker buses with the same apparently loudmouth children on them,
whether I'm in the stooshness of St. John's Wood or the openness of an
open-top tour bus at the top of Park Lane or on the 56 going towards *murder mile*

or even somewhere like.... God-forbid... Croydon
I get the same voices trying their best in the same old way to shatter the
silence.

Message:

~~There is no room here~~
Not enough room here to deflect your questions

But we still speak on the
Phone:
Your voice sounds more distant, more monotone
and my inflected accent is harder for you to decipher
and there are more spaces than words, and my voice has got quieter

Because I find it hard to speak when bitter love songs play on the speaker van which is driving round the town.

Bachata on the radio station: *Si no te tengo, que se me venga el mundo encima (If I don't have you/ may my whole world cave in on me)*

See, if this were London, I could shut up and shut down with my new lily-white earphones inside my ears. I don't want to hear... I don't want to think

I could blend in behind the pollution, the sound of cars and motorbikes and breaking glass next door, young couples screaming at each other on either side... us screaming at each other, remember?

I could blend in behind fear of crime, gated communities clinking shut, lost identity cards dropping from stolen handbags, our identities lost in the middle of the latest ringtones being tested out by the people on the seat behind

The t-t-tinny sound of dance music
The heavy B-b-bass sound of "urban" music
The foot stomping on my ceiling telling me to
TURN IT DOWN
Turn it down

All the same
Silence

Email:
Re: You asked me what I miss?

I'm booking the ticket home
back to wrapping myself in layers, back to overpriced bedsits and uncertainty

Baseballs are whizzing above me and the generator's throbbing because the
power's out again

Back home I must renegotiate the languages I was once familiar with:
txts, Teletext, subtext, bad language, sign language and the hundreds of
foreign languages that populate train carriages

They all amount to silence because, if I'm not careful, I'll find myself
apologising for coughing on the tube journey in.

Because, if I am careful, I'll forget to talk about what I miss
amidst the shoulder-shrug, half-smile, no-you-go-first gestures, accompanied
by a subtle wink.

I wonder whether I will change my mind…
but I can't hear my doubts over my heartbeat.

What it's like to be named after your father... (draft 1.5)

I

It is just one small syllable to swallow
one giant twenty-year leap to digest
one that takes a split-second to spit
but falls heavy and splits

into two nicknames
from three siblings
in-jokes traced back
to days you couldn't spell.

It is for not being that pianist, it is for not being named
after that pianist
it is for not being named
just echoed.

It is five letters that stand:
for being little on days you feel big
for being Junior on days you feel old
for being second when you do not thirst
for hand-me-downs
And for the –y stitched on to the end.

It is growing up with sliced-open mail
even when you have grown to be the last male
in a house of six.

II

Here is what comes

after hoping for apples to fall far from the branches that bore them

after hoping for strong breezes

and after still always falling flat-faced onto the same old chip-block copy shop

floor

after waiting to grow into your face

after waiting for your face to grow in the same wide-scalped way

and after mirrors, forecasting things to come one hair-follicle at a time

Here is becoming

resigned to your inheritance

learning to love those who mouth you

in differently-flavoured tones.

Here is being too slippery

to hold onto a name

but still trying to grip

each letter

with your teeth:

it is still one giant leap

to hope _____.

Crepe Paper Hats

They asked me if I had a Christmas poem
So I said... *Ho ho ho no!*
I cannot not mince my words into pie-sized sound bytes
I get bored of these charades
Find it too hard a task
For you to ask me to cast a jingly glow over my words to mask
The serious word play crocheted into its foundation

My words are not turkeys to stuff full of James Bond clichés
Reruns of Star Wars
Or Home Alone 1, 2, 3, 4... and how many more before we realise
It isn't that entertaining watching mothers abandon their children over
Christmas
Especially when you're a child who just wants to be left alone?

But if this were to be a Christmas poem
I'd say this isn't just *any* Christmas poem
This is a choice selection
Of cluedo, monopoly, monotony
And a lobotomising litany of all the films you've ever seen since you were five
Like the Never-Ending Story has really never ended
Just waited for you to return one year later to the bum-shaped dent on your
mother's sofa
You created at the beginning of time

Only each year it gets wider
Like your [*insert relative*]'s yawning mouth as she reaches out

With her bingo wings to retrieve another glass of Bailey's

This isn't just *any* Christmas poem
This is a carefully basted cut-and-pasted
Stitch-work of all the ghosts of Christmases past and present
That present itself annually...
Like the present they keep asking after
Like how are you to say you left the sweater
On the tube the following day?
But yes you *really* love it! And pink is *so* your colour!

This isn't just *any* Christmas poem
This poem should be hanging off trees
And dancing in drunken office dos
Releasing itself from the grip of tongues
Loosened by libidinous Lambrini
And peach schnapps

This poem is more polished that the Queen's Speech
More out of reach than those Ferrero Rochers way up above the cupboard
Your mother had been leaving for a special occasion

This poem, as violently sudden as an invasion of bombs on Lebanon
As a boxing day hangover looms
And your brother enters the room and says lets switch off the news:
Your nephew wants to watch cartoons

This poem should be a Carol
A lullaby and hallelujah nativity scene

Printed on a last-minute card
You forgot to send before the last Christmas post

This poem is a ghost of white baby Jesuses
Decorating the walls in the Halal burger bar

This poem should be a Carol
Although if it has to be a man
It should be a Cliff
Hanging onto the charts with a dodgy rendition of
[sung] *Our Father Who Art In Heaven, Hallowed Be Thy Name...*
And if Pussy Riot can be jailed for defaming Christ
Then we should let Sir Cliff Richard suffer the same

This poem is a shameful gluttonous, overrated, belly-bloating
Feast you need to sink your teeth into

And this poem isn't just any Christmas poem
And if it were to continue
You would have to release another notch on your belt
Ease yourself down into your chair
Borrow a pair of reindeer antennae
And tune in to the tinny tinge of tinselated references
Injected into its rump

But I shall leave this poem here as just a stump
An unwanted turkey drumstick chucked out
Onto the (Only Way Is) Essex asphalt
An unwanted burp emanating from a mouth that has already said too much

Drunk too much

Been fed too much

And as such, before I venture into territory I dare not tread

I shall leave this poem here

Like a crepe paper hat hanging over an embarrassed head

#outro/bonustracks

Last few words peace

You've been writing...

You've been writing poetry again
I can spot that leaky pen on your lip
From miles away
And your tongue with the stale taste of metaphor still on
Which you've tried to brush away
Pah! The verses linger still in your kiss

You've been writing poetry again
Don't worry, I can tell
It's that fingertip smell
The keyboard stain
The pinky poised above delete
Pushing out your veins

Why this vain obsession?
Lines layered with double meaning
And painstakingly revised
Which you pat into shape
And stanzardise
If words are your food
Why do you play with them
Why do you use them for tools to confuse and condense?

You've been writing that intense poetry again
There's a rhyme in your mind
And a line in your eyes that I can trace

I can see it in your face

'Cause there's a rhythm that you're tapping

And it's not mine

You've been writing that poetry

Yeah, I know you by now

I can hear it in your diction

Your dirty addiction to watching couplets form

The smile as a simile emerges

Your urges to splurge your emotions

Onto innocent sheets

You've been at it again, I lie?

It's the tell-tale tic of your head

As puns pull up seats on your screen

The debris of undeveloped phrases

Onto pages

As you spit feeling into words

And shuffle meanings into verse

You've been injecting rhythm into those lines

You're just a meter away from lunacy

And it's pathetic the way you're dressing things up in imagery

And symbolism

Because let's face it

You're just inventing new rhymes

And new ways

To say the same old things

Like you're in love

Or like you're scared
Or like you're angry
Like you're confused

Because you don't understand life's rules
So you use a poem as a ruse
To redraft them into metrical form
And this isn't normal

No, this isn't normal at all

P.S.

You've been writing on walls
Instead of fighting in wars
Your Bic-gripping hands
Should be handling concrete grit
You should grit your teeth and grin and bear shit
You should be more functional
You should be more like your brother
You should be less of a dreamer
You should be cleaner
More productive

So shut down your PC junk
Put down your dictionary
Pack up your pens
And close your books
Unsquint your eyes and look

Look out at the world

Go on, brave the cold daylight

Of the outside

Without the cloak of allusion

Without the joke of your delusional imagery

Without the hope of a metaphor or simile

Without the seasoning of rhyme

To waste your time

You should be ashamed

Of doing the strange things to language that you do

While the Earth still turns

While cities riot and burn

You must learn

That life is not a blank page

For you to scrawl your doo-doo ideas on

Because there are too many wrongs to write

So goodnight

Before You Leave (Parting Words)

Before you leave

Remember that these streets don't owe you

Remember that these paving slabs are just stepping stones

For you to find a path back home

But don't let the railings keep you boxed in

Forge your own way

And don't be led astray

By the sway of thick hips

Or by lips with quick-talk

Or by eyes wide with promises

That can never be fulfilled

Be strong-willed

But softly-spoken

And keep your mind open

Even if it gets filled with junk

Cos ideas are for recycling

Before you leave

Remember that these streets don't own you

And you don't own them

For your time on Earth is on loan

And you walk it alone

Although you share the pavement

With those that you love

But don't be chained to these streets

Don't let them claim you

For you may think you're "on road"

But you are not your postcode

So don't let signposts contain you

Let them guide you to the destination you choose

Don't let your shoes get bogged down

With the rhythm of this town

And don't wear your sole out

By treading the same ground

Before you leave

Remember that these streets don't know you

Like you know them

For their routes are mapped out

But yours are fresh with every breath

And the complexity of your thoughts

Are more vibrant than any city

And only you can navigate your way through

So use your heart as a compass

And your spirit as an atlas

And you'll lose yourself

And find yourself again

And you will learn that the race

Is about being on the track

Not just about winning

Before you leave

Remember not to pack

All of my pedestrian advice into your emotional baggage

Lest it be heavy on your back

For you will find your own pathway home

You will inhabit your own space

And find your own place

And when you do

I hope that you do not lock the gate

To your heart

Even if you aren't awaiting guests

For many good things happen from what we don't expect

Just remember that you are loved

That you are more perfect

Than the neighbourhoods that raised you

That there are avenues

Waiting for you to walk through

But you must search for them

For these streets do not owe you promises

Nor do you own their secrets

Nor do they know your depths

As you negotiate your steps

And steer your own way

Before you leave

Remember to stand tall

For you are loved

Remember that others may follow your footprints

So walk good

And step true

When you're making your way through

To whatever destination that you have in your mind

I hope you find that these parting words serve you well.

CPSIA information can be obtained
at www.ICGtesting.com
Printed in the USA
LVHW06s1250030718
582586LV00011B/134/P